MAST MARKETING FOR STARTERS

THE BRIEF GUIDE TO B2B MARKETING AND SALES

Including the methods, tricks and processes for every step

Jeffrey Coleman

Summary

—

Introduction

By choosing to read this book, I already know a few things about you. You made the decision to pick up a nonfiction book on new client generation, while others chose to waste their time on distractions that would only provide them with short term gratification. This one decision will put you ahead of others, and it's this kind of decision that will propel your company or career to levels others will never reach. As a consultant, I can tell you that I've only come across two types of people in business; those that constantly learn so they can get an edge, and those that don't. I already know who's who by the type of project I get asked to be a part of. The fast-growing companies that want to get bigger, faster, and stronger just happen to be run by executives who constantly read and want an edge over their competition. The companies that are struggling and desperately need life pumped into them to survive are usually run by people that haven't had any new ideas in a while, and have been coasting in business (and life). I don't believe it's a coincidence. Those that are constantly growing and looking for an edge, eat the lunch of those who coast and hope for the best.

There's no judgment in my voice when I say this, I'm just stating facts. And for those of you who think that nothing's so black and white, that there are more categories in business than just growing or dying, there aren't. There are varying degrees of these two states, but make no mistake, if you are not growing in life or business you are dying. You're either moving up or being pulled down. There are no plateaus. Plateaus are a myth. If you're not burning fuel and fighting gravity to climb higher, that gravity is pulling you down and will do so until you crash. In business that gravity is called attrition.

When your business isn't bringing in new clients and it's living off your existing customer base, it is slowly dying. One by one your clients are getting picked off by competitors. Some customers move to a different area, so they're forced to find a new vendor. Others go out of business. Maybe someone in your customer service department pissed a customer off, so they decide to never do business with you again, just to prove a point. Or maybe, it's just that your client's nephew now sells similar services and they feel obligated to give the business to their family member. There are thousands of reasons customers leave and they all happen over time. Which means time is working for you, if you're generating new customers, or time is working against you, slowly killing your business.

Attrition isn't only killing your customer base. It's going after your products, your people, and everything associated with your business. Products

—

7

that aren't constantly updated with more bells and whistles are getting crushed by products that are. The iPhone changed the mobile phone industry forever, and yet if you were to use the first version of the iPhone today, I'm sure you'd want to throw it in the garbage in frustration, because so much has evolved since that first iteration. How about your employees? They couldn't regress, could they? Your people are either getting sharper with continual training, or they're getting rusty because they haven't gone through training in a while. The reality is that we can't even say that a business, as a whole, is growing or dying because those who are at the top of their market know that they need to examine every individual component of the business and make sure that there is progress. Don't be fooled by activity or change. Anyone can keep themselves busy, and change is inevitable, but progress is forward movement.

When you're aiming for progress, the very first place to look is your client acquisition strategy. Without a constant flow of new clients, nothing else matters. The success or failure of your business starts with your ability to bring in new business. In helping organizations of all different shapes and sizes, in a wide array of industries, I can definitively tell you that one of the most common problems in sales is lack of structure. Specifically, most organizations lack a structured process that they can repeat over and over, to generate new clients again and again. And even large corporations that have carefully built a process can suffer because only some salespeople follow it, and only some of the time. This leaves large companies with the same disadvantage small and midsize companies have: not being able to generate new customers and clients on demand.

Many salespeople are just left to themselves to figure things out. Not only are business owners not supporting their salespeople, but what's worse, they are relying on salespeople to supply the formula for bringing in business. Since business owners and executives are struggling to figure out how to get more clients and bring in more accounts, they search for the answer by sifting through more and more resumes in the hopes that if they can just find a salesperson with enough experience, that person will come with the solution they need, or at least contacts that can be leveraged to generate new business. But what comes next when neither the salesperson nor management has a process that can consistently bring in new accounts? What happens when those contacts are exhausted? When no one has answers and the well has run dry, those salespeople are eventually let go, or they quit because they know it's eventually coming.

Turnover is extremely expensive, and what I just described is completely backwards. Just like all business processes, it's management's responsibility to ensure that the organization has a strong sales process in place and to ensure that all the salespeople are supported in their efforts. Salespeople should be given constant training on that process and supplied with all the tools they need to thrive. This way, the fate of the organization is not in the hands of the sales team. Management leads, the team follows. Now if you're a one-person organization, you can use this methodology to rapidly grow your business and then standardize the practices that you set, so that others can follow. If you are a salesperson reading this book, then use this methodology to become the top producer at your organization. When no one understands how you are getting the results you're getting, you may be asked to implement this for the entire team.

So, what is the big promise? This book will show you how to consistently generate new clients without having to cold call, tediously create content, or spend a dollar on advertising. I will show you how to develop a full client acquisition system that generates new clients on demand, whether you are doing this for yourself or for your organization with thousands of salespeople. Client Machine is written for those that want that advantage I described earlier. It's written for those of you who value working smarter over working harder and would rather save years of time and lost opportunity while trying to figure it out on your own.

What makes this book unique among sales books is the two perspectives it is written from. The first perspective comes from my experience as a business growth consultant, where my work is focused on creating structure and building processes to help companies move faster and grow more rapidly.

Companies don't get far without standardized processes, because everyone moves in different directions. Without structure, scaling is impossible. Since your goal isn't just to learn something new, but to take your business to the next level, this first perspective is vital to your achieving results. This holds true whether 'your business' means your sales numbers if you're a salesperson, or your total revenue if you're the CEO. The second perspective comes from my fascination with, and years of research on topics like psychology, influence and persuasion, NLP, sales and marketing. I've had the privilege of working closely with experts like the master of persuasion himself, Dr. Kevin Hogan, author of 24 books and best known for his internationally bestselling classic, The Psychology of Persuasion: How to Persuade Others to Your Way of Thinking. For the last 22 years I've been obsessed with learning how we're wired and how we make decisions, in order to understand why we do what we do. I've taken the knowledge I've accumulated throughout my journey and designed a sales process that taps into how buying decisions are made. A process that can rapidly increase your sales pipeline, shorten your sales cycles, and generate all the clients you want. Big promise? Now it's time to deliver.

Creating a Solid Foundation for Revenue Growth

Does Your B2B Revenue Strategy Need a Tune-up or a Transformation? - Six Key Indicators

To be successful at growing revenue, you need to first define the scope of the issue. Sometimes you go to the doctor with an issue, and he or she says something like, "You need to lose a few pounds, so cut back on the sugar." At other, less fortunate times, your doc may say something such as, "We found a serious problem, and we need to put you on an aggressive treatment program right now" ("stat," in medical vernacular).

We rarely treat marketing and sales issues, and the need for revenue growth, as a life or death situation; however, to your company and mine, the concept is the same. There is almost always something we can do to improve revenue health. But the big question is – are your challenges chronic, because they have been occurring over a long period of time, or are they acute – because they are now severe or intense?

We often let the chronic problems go and learn to live with less than our best. In this case, the acute problems are sometimes more helpful because they force us to confront the issues.

With medical problems, very poor health can lead us to make changes that propel us to better health. Exactly the same is true in our search for revenue. Crisis points can become growth catalysts.

ust to add to this point, there are companies who were riding high and considered to be almost unbeatable industry leaders; yet, they had chronic issues that were not properly addressed. Examples of such companies include Blackberry, Word Perfect, Blockbuster, Xerox, Myspace, AOL, and Yahoo. All of these firms, and hundreds/thousands of lesser known examples, had chronic issues to start. When not addressed, they turned into acute conditions that could not be overcome.

Here are six questions we take our clients through when determining the scope of their revenue growth effort. Spend a bit of time considering your answers because it will help as you read through the action steps to follow.

1. What is your current trajectory? By trajectory, I mean the path you are on and whether you are going in the right or wrong direction. Trajectory can be expressed both in qualitative

and quantitative terms. Do you feel confident about where the direction of your company is going, or do you have that gnawing feeling that you are off course? Are your key performance indicators (KPIs), like revenue growth, average transaction size, profitability, sales conversion rations, opportunities, leads and awareness on target or starting to decline?

2. Is your business model aligned with the future or the past? I recently read an interesting AdAge article about Scott Olrich, CMO of DocuSign. Olrich talks about how he is always thinking not just about where his company is today, but more importantly, where his business category is going. Olrich is correct in that failure to look forward can be an anchor on success. We saw this in the software industry. Many software companies neglected the shift to the cloud (then called SaaS) until swifter and more flexible start-ups took a huge

market share away from the once-mighty giants.

3. Is your branding stale or fresh? Good branding is a hallmark of an effective marketing and sales program, and we have seen many examples of companies that benefited from a rebranding exercise. But how do you know whether your branding needs a refresh or a redo? Here are a few questions to complete a quick self-diagnostic on the relevance and freshness of your brand:

4. Is our brand crystal clear to prospects?

5. Are we differentiated from our competitors?

6. Are we perceived as we want to be?

7. Does our brand reflect where we have been or where we are going?

8. Does our staff feel proud of our branding and messaging?

9. Do you have the right team on board? I hope that you have the best people to get you to the

next level of revenue growth; however, if your current team is lacking in attitude or aptitude, this is an area you will definitely need to address sooner rather than later. It is particularly important to make sure any team additions have not only good technical skills, but also valid experience in your forward-looking business model.

10.   Do you have a solid lead-to-revenue (L2R) framework? Your L2R framework consists of all the processes, tools, and people involved in each step, from initial awareness to close of the business. You should not only document each process, but capture relevant metrics such as cost per sale, lead conversion ratios, close rates, etc. Much more about this later.

11.   Are you willing to make necessary changes? This is perhaps the most important question of all, and the above questions are not

worth pondering if you are not willing to take action based on your answers. As this cartoon suggests, whether you need a revenue growth tune-up or a transformation program, waiting for better results to occur without action on your part is just a form of "magical thinking."

**"What if we don't change at all ...
and something magical just happens."**

Whether your needed change is of the short-term, tune-up variety or a complete transformation of your brand, business model and lead-to-revenue framework – things do not get better by themselves. Act now; get on the right trajectory, and reap the benefits.

The Innovation Imperative

In his excellent article titled, An Open Letter to CEOs, Alex Osterwalder, co-founder of @Strategyzer, reported, "A recent McKinsey study shows that 80% of your CEO peers think that their current business model is at risk. The research also shows that a mere 6% of your executives are satisfied with the innovation process in your organization."

While these statistics sound foreboding, I believe this anxiety about the future, if not taken to extremes, can be healthy. Andrew Grove's book title said it all, Only the Paranoid Survive. And the time to be paranoid is before your competitors take market share and before you become obsolete in your product, service delivery, or in your messaging.

Earlier in my career, I was part of several companies that failed to prepare for the onslaught of the SaaS/cloud software model. One of these firms was a leader in the CRM space that could have launched a cloud version (protecting their flank) while continuing to upgrade the installed version (protecting the core business). Their failure to do so cost the company hundreds of millions in valuation. I wish that I had been more forceful at the time, but the CEO insisted that customers would be fine with the installed version. Wrong!

When it comes to major innovations, private companies have one advantage over public companies – they do not have to report quarterly earnings to maintain or grow the stock price. I have been in the executive meetings where decisions were based more on meeting the expectations of financial analysts and stockholders (e.g. quarterly earnings) than on investing in a better future. This may be a useful strategy for the short-term but not so much for long-term growth and sustainability.

No one said that being a leader is supposed to be easy. You have to keep everything moving forward in the core business, while continually figuring out how to beat competitors who may not even exist. Here are some ideas on how to accomplish this:

- Separate the innovators from the sustainers. There are talented employees in your company who are good at keeping things on track. They build the products, service the customers, manage the books, hire and administer the staff, and so forth. However, these sustainers can be like a deer in the headlights when it comes to innovation and will do their best to stifle the new idea if it threatens the status quo.

- Go for the big win. Sure, you can innovate on little things, like a subtle change in pricing strategy or some new product features. But, why not go for the big win - the 2x, 3x or 10x improvement - to pull away from the competition.

- Never take your success for granted. If you are tempted to do so, think about yesterday's seemingly unbeatable market leaders such as, Kodak, Sun Microsystems, Sears, Blockbuster, Nokia, and Blackberry. Also keep in mind that only 71 companies remain today from the original 1955 Fortune 500 list.

- Organize to embrace innovation. I have seen instances where "innovation" was no more than one of the so-called company values listed on a coffee mug. The organizations that claim to support innovation don't have to talk about it; they live it. They give space for people to make mistakes and don't keep pulling the innovators back to the core business every time they hit a bump in the quarterly numbers.

- Allow for controversy. As Margaret Heffernan said in her Ted Talk, Daring to Disagree, "For good ideas and true innovation, you need human interaction, conflict, argument, debate."

Innovation Examples

Dollar Shave Club: Great example of taking an entrepreneurial approach to an established business model. Instead of buying razors at a retail outlet, you now subscribe to receive them monthly. The company was acquired by Unilever for about $1 billion and now has 3.2 million members.

Zipcar: This innovative company's motto is: OWN THE TRIP, NOT THE CAR™ – You drive, and we'll take care of the rest. Members apply online and are issued a Zipcard, which is used to access vehicles worldwide. You then search for a nearby car and reserve it for as little as one hour. The Zipcard is used to unlock the car, and the keys are inside. Just drop off the car when you are done.

MSC Industrial Supply Co.: This Company jumped from the traditional model of industrial sales in 2000 by launching MSCDirect.com as its eCommerce site. Since that time, they have grown online sales to 60 percent of total revenue ($1.6 billion out of $2.9 billion). As an example of not abandoning its past, the company maintained its staff of woodworking specialists who meet with customers, onsite. MSC won the B2B E-Commerce Player of the Year Award at the Internet Retailer Excellence Awards in June 2016.

Deere & Co.: One of the oldest of the old-line companies, the John Deere folks are not relying on past successes. They are making a major expansion into B2B eCommerce, with a heavy focus on supporting mobile applications. For example, their MyMaintenance application lets customers view and document maintenance schedules by calendar or by how many hours a particular piece of equipment has been used. The application links directly to the ordering system by sending alerts allowing customers to buy parts and installation service –a benefit to customers to be sure, but also good for Deere & Co.'s bottom line.

I've mostly covered innovation as it pertains to large companies because these are the examples with which we are familiar. But what is true for these large companies is just as true for micro businesses and the small-to-medium business (SMB) market. Regardless of the size or your company, you must adapt to survive and innovate to thrive.

Building the Foundation

This book is broken up into three sections; Foundation, Lead Generation Machine, and Sales Machine. Client Machine is a combination of two powerful individual processes that come together perfectly to systematically generate clients in line with what you can handle. It consists of building a lead generation machine that repeatedly fills your calendar with sales appointments, and a Sales Machine that converts those prospects to new clients. To effectively grow and scale your business, you must strategically build these two machines on a strong foundation. The first section is dedicated to showing you how to operate in a way that uses your resources wisely to get the highest return on your investments. These resources are your time, money, energy, team, technology and so on.

This book is aimed at salespeople, executives, and business owners alike. There's something, in fact many things, for everyone. Parts of this first section on foundation are written with the business owner and executive in mind, since they're the ones with the power to make structural changes in the organization. I also strongly urge salespeople to read this section and resist the temptation to jump right into lead generation and the sales process. There are plenty of valuable insights that you'd miss out by skipping ahead. You may also find yourself in a position to implement these strategies in your organization. Creating a client machine without a sufficient foundation will severely limit your potential.

Customers Vs Clients

Before we begin, let's differentiate between the word customer and client. The word customer is defined as anyone who purchases goods or services from another. 'Customers' are often associated with transactional purchases; simple, short-term sales where the customer already knows what he or she needs, and where very little effort is required from the salesperson. On the other side of the spectrum, a client is defined as one that is under the protection or patronage of another; a dependent. 'Clients' are often associated with solution selling, which is a more complex process, involving the collaboration of both buyer and seller, in which the latter must first develop an understanding of the client's business, industry, and needs, in order to design a solution that solves problems and achieves their objectives. Since clients are more dependent on the person advising them, they tend to be much more loyal than customers. And since the value they receive is perceived to be much higher than the value a customer would get from a transactional sale, clients pay more money. Regardless of what industry you're in, or how you currently describe your buyer, going forward you should consider them all to be clients. Simply adopting this label immediately defines your role and responsibilities, and instructs you to deliver in a way where you are valued more, and consequently paid more. That additional value comes from the added service of becoming their advisor. It's no longer about you selling a product or service; it's about you solving their problem. You're guiding them through their challenges, navigating through the rough waters to get them to safety. The experience you bring, the guidance you provide, and the comfort you supply during these challenging times is the value you bring and the premium you are paid. Imagine, a sales process so good that not only do you close more deals, but clients are happier, and you are paid a premium because of it? Since price correlates with value, this book will show you how to do just that.

Inbound Vs Outbound

Whenever I'm asked, "What should I do? What's better, inbound or outbound marketing?" I typically respond: "Would you rather have your left arm or your right arm?" After the initial confused look, the response to that is, "Well I'd rather have both to be honest". And that is the ultimate answer. But first let's understand where this division came from in the first place. Marketing automation software companies like Hubspot were responsible for coining the term 'inbound marketing', and more importantly, they were also responsible for creating this inbound vs outbound environment in their clever marketing campaigns. Software like theirs was initially created to help businesses capitalize on incoming traffic and the leads generated from it.

To help create a path for the prospect to go through, making the buying journey a positive experience and nurturing those leads until the prospect was ready to act. The truth is, this was desperately needed because most leads were being wasted by Sales and a CRM alone wasn't enough.

Companies were spending a fortune generating those leads only to find out that their salespeople would call once and never follow up. One study showed that on average, salespeople were only calling leads 1.3 times, and most of those attempts ended with the salesperson never actually getting the prospect on the phone. Marketing automation software combined with CRM's allowed companies to keep track of the leads, prioritize them, and create predetermined workflows for the sales teams to follow so that each lead was given exactly what was needed to help them move to the next stage of buying.

This was all well and good, except for one minor detail; this process assumed that your website had all this traffic in the first place. It worked for larger companies that had a brand name and were spending a ton of money on advertising. But it was completely useless to everyone else. What good is triggered email or creating a lead score if you're a small business with no incoming leads? It was pointless.

As the technology got more sophisticated and marketing automation companies started popping up all over, they had to create a bigger pie instead of constantly dividing the existing one.

To do this they had to create the need for their product, which they did by teaching small business owners how to drive traffic to their website. In turn, small business owners would then need marketing automation software, continuing the growth of this industry and developing a new norm for marketers.

White papers were created, along with videos, infographics, and blog posts on how we should be creating content, so you could get the prospect to come to you as opposed to going after the prospect directly. They created this inbound vs outbound argument that said outbound is old school, tacky, and no longer worked. We were told that we would be bothering people if we approached them through outbound, that we'd be looked at as disruptive and disrespectful.

The timing of this propaganda couldn't have been more perfect. There was a major transition that was happening at the time.

See, during the period right before that time, direct mail was a significant form of prospecting, but costs were increasing. As postage was increasing, long distance calling rates were rapidly decreasing until they eventually disappeared, thanks to unlimited calling packages through the internet.

This created an environment where prospectors got most of their business by cold calling on the telephone. Just like everything else that gets saturated, prospects started getting more and more frustrated with these cold calls all day long, while salespeople were getting burnt out speaking to frustrated people all day, or worse, not getting through at all because gatekeepers were getting increasingly better at not letting any sales calls through. Right on cue, in comes the message that says outbound is evil, old school, and no longer works... BOOM... you have a whole new generation believing that it's better to have the prospect come to you.

Obviously, there are benefits having a prospect come to you, but there were many misleading factors in this argument, as well as other important considerations which were left out in making the case for inbound over outbound. So, let's go back to the choice of having one arm or another. I say I prefer both, just like inbound and outbound. But, if I were forced to pick one, that's easy - my strong arm! Now let me quickly explain why outbound is the strong arm.

People are drowning in content. With everyone saturating the market with their content, prospects can't possibly consume this much. With so much information being generated and the majority of it low quality because marketers think it's a race in quantity, your prospects aren't even reading your stuff.

Inbound marketing costs too much.

Regardless of what they tell you in cost per lead, I will show you how to get the lowest cost, highest quality lead through outbound. Your competitors are writing articles, creating infographics, filming videos, and now even live streaming their messages, so you'd have to have a team of people constantly creating content just to stand out from all of the other content being published. Not only is this very costly, but in my opinion it's like screaming louder and louder in a room that is progressively getting noisier.

It takes too much time. Think about planting seed after seed hoping that enough seeds are planted so that you can reap the rewards over time.

An effective content strategy can take 12-18 months before it blossoms into consistent leads. If you think about live streaming, that's information that disappears after the livestream is over.

Because the content game is so competitive, it's becoming more demanding.

In order to compete, you now have to provide your information in real time, only for that information to be discarded after the livestream is over. At least a video is an asset that can be used repeatedly. With outbound you can get a lead, or even a new customer, tomorrow!

Inbound leads are terrible. Decision-makers don't research a list of vendors to choose from, nor are they the ones walking around tradeshows.

High level decision-makers usually pass off these tasks to lower level employees, which means your sales team is spending all their time with people who can't make the YES decision, but who can easily make the NO decision by not including your company in their list of possibilities.

You can't go above these people's heads because you risk creating an enemy instead of a champion, which means that you have to rely on them selling for you by passing your message on.

The only issue there is that after you've given them a 45-minute demonstration of how your products or services will solve all their problems, this employee will, in turn, give a condensed, 3-minute summary to the decision-maker!

Let me briefly take you into the world of strategic outbound. You can identify which type of companies would feel the greatest positive impact from your products/services. You can create a list of companies that mirrors your biggest or best clients and go after them. You won't have to hope that the right type of company finds you. Let's think about all the hoping you would have to do. You would have to hope that:

- The perfect company (biggest profit potential or biggest impact) would recognize that they have a specific problem you solve.
- After recognizing they have that problem, they would believe the type of solution you provide

is the answer to that problem. For example, if I think I don't have as much sales as I should have, there are many different solutions for this. I can look for sales trainers, want to hire more salespeople, look to purchase software, research 100 different marketing strategies, etc. But let's say the perfect company recognizes they need a solution like yours. You would have to hope that...

- They stumble upon your content as opposed to someone else's.
- The content was so good it converted that prospect to a lead.
- And after all that... you're hoping that the person doing this happens to be the ultimate decision-maker.
- With strategic outbound you can:

- Generate a list of the most desirable target companies.

- Target the actual decision-makers.

- Do your research on them and their company before contacting them.

- Bring a problem to them in such a way that if they didn't previously realize it existed, now they will.

- Provide specific solutions based on industry experience and company research.

- Create awareness, interest, and desire so that they take action.

- Don't let inbound marketers confuse you.

Outbound marketing is not the same as mass marketing.

The old-school methods of 'spray and pray' mass marketing are not welcome anywhere, but laser-targeted strategic outbound can bring you immediate sales tomorrow. I want to wrap up this topic by giving you a new view on outbound, a different perspective than the, "Outbound is too disruptive - You're bothering people" mentality that has been lingering in this politically correct new world.

If I'd just found the cure to Cancer and knew my uncle, who I love, has been dealing with a lot going through it, you are damn right that I would disrupt whatever he was doing to let him know!

I wouldn't care what he was in the middle of; I would feel obligated to immediately make him stop what he was doing and tell him the great news. He's in the middle of eating dinner with the family? Great, put me on speaker phone because everyone is going to love hearing the great news!

In no way am I suggesting that it's okay for you to wake your clients up at 5 a.m. or disrupt their dinner just because you're excited about your product, or that you think they should listen to your sales pitch. What I am saying is that if you truly have a fix for your prospect's biggest challenge and can provide information which will greatly impact their business, you have an obligation to bring it to their attention. For example, if I know that a prospect is struggling with getting new business and I know that they are hurting financially because they don't have an effective process in place, I'm not going to just sit there and let them die. When I have a simple solution that can mean millions of dollars in revenue for them, literally change their business, and provide a stable environment for their employees, I'm not going to stand by and hope that someone at that company stumbles across my content and reaches out to me. The right partnership means that it will benefit both parties, which means that it would be irresponsible for me not to approach them. It would be irresponsible to both of us.

I brought up the politically correct environment because it amazes me how so many people are so scared of causing offence they end up doing more damage by not helping. They're more concerned about ruining a relationship that doesn't even exist yet, just with the idea that someone might get offended by the approach.

I can tell you that this mindset won't allow anyone to survive in business. If you start with a great product or service that you're so proud of that you feel the obligation to bring it right to the door of every man, woman, child on this earth so they can benefit from it, you will have a solid foundation.

As a salesperson you have to fall in love with your product or service, or don't sell it.

You won't be good at selling something that you think is anything short of amazing.

If you're a business owner or executive, make sure that your team is innovating and working each day to make your product or service better. For those who provide a service that can't be innovated, then make sure your team gets better at delivering it, or differentiate yourself by catering to the client in a way that no one else does. This book isn't about your products or services. It assumes you already have a great mousetrap. That's just the starting point. This book will show you how to take these great offerings and use them to systematically build new client relationships.

Pitch the Niche

When we talk about a niche, this is one of those lessons that you already know but probably aren't following, or at least not to the extent you could. I love teaching things that someone already knows because we save time by not having to prove the concept. Implementation happens faster. I'll give you my perspective on niches anyway, just to build more leverage on following through, but my hope for you is that by the end of this topic you're excited about this principle and ready to take it to the next level in all your sales and marketing campaigns going forward.

When slow or no growth companies ask me for help, the first place I look is to see if they've chosen a niche to operate in or not. Companies that don't choose a niche to dominate never dominate anything and therefore struggle.

This struggle comes from a fear that committing to

one market may alienate other business that falls outside that market. In turn they try to be all things to all people, rarely becoming anything to anyone. Let me ask you who you would choose if you needed heart surgery? Would you go to your general practitioner or a heart surgeon? The choice is obvious. Now let's try something less dramatic. Imagine there's a dispute over your product name and now there's possible trademark infringement litigation. And, as luck would have it, you're also in the process of going through a divorce and need to hire an attorney. Would you use the same person for both? Probably not. Even if they assured you they were experienced in both areas, chances are you would look for both the best intellectual property attorney you could find (however you define best), and also the divorce attorney that best meets your needs. In fact, if someone told you that they had a lot of experience in both matters, you probably wouldn't think they were fully competent in either area.

Understanding Time, Speed, and Growth

The real power in picking a niche is how it affects the speed at which things happen. See, growth is important, but velocity determines the size of your company and the options you have for future decisions. Ultimately, velocity not only impacts but controls your destiny. Let me explain what I mean with a visual. Let's suppose your company falls into one of the buckets below. For demonstration purposes, let's say that your company generates just under $5M in annual sales, which means that it will be found in bucket A.

If your company does that same $5M in sales, except this time you get that done in only 6 months instead of 12, now your company is on track to do $10M a year in sales and you'd be in bucket B. Taking that example further, if you can hit those $5M in sales in only 3 months' time and do this every quarter, you've now moved to bucket C. Like I said, the significance of these revenues goes far beyond my buckets in this demonstration. A company in bucket C is taken far more seriously than bucket A and has many more resources to create more product lines, enter new markets, acquire companies, and therefore multiply faster.

Now that we understand the importance of speed, let's dig a little deeper to discover the two main areas of speed you need to focus on to achieve rapid growth.

The speed of making a sale.

This involves any and every sale, from acquiring a new customer to upselling and cross selling. The faster you can convert clients and generate new sales, the faster you can start working on the next one. Think about all the time it takes to follow up and get the person on the telephone or try to coordinate an in-person meeting. Meetings can be pushed back days, and often weeks at a time. If you add up that time, accounting for all the prospects and existing clients you deal with throughout the year, what would that wasted time amount to? More importantly, how much more business would you have if you used that wasted time to generate more clients? If you have a sales team, that number just multiplied.

The speed of delivering the goods or services.

This is your back end. Your company has a certain capacity and it's important that your front-end sales machine isn't bringing in more business than you can deliver from the back end. As much as it seems like it's a good problem to have, it isn't. This is where customers become dissatisfied and leave you. Not only do they never come back, and you forever lose their business, but it creates a long ripple effect of lost revenue. Dissatisfied customers hurt your reputation on their way out, robbing you of additional future revenue.

When you're not able to properly deliver on your offering, whether that means physically delivering a product, or performing to the level you promised, you create a ton of work for yourself (or others) in dealing with an unhappy customer.

And every minute you spend communicating with a customer about a prior purchase you're no longer getting paid from, decreases the profitability of that transaction. Conversations of this nature require time and energy from you or your team, and when you burn these resources on completed transactions, it removes focus from delivering to new paying customers, affecting both your output and revenue. Your goal is to be able to deliver your value to that customer in an exceptional way through to completion, so you can move on to the next one. If you do this effectively, the only need for additional conversations would be because the customer is considering additional purchases.

These two items should be focal points for your entire operation.

Regardless of what you sell, think of your business as a manufacturing company which must produce and deliver, over and over again.

On the front end you're manufacturing clients and producing sales. The initial raw materials to manufacture clients are a list of names of prospects, scheduled on your calendar, and the information that you have to help them. Through your manufacturing process, this list of names goes into your client machine on one end and on the other side a new client is created, and a transaction is produced. Your goal is to follow this process repeatedly, producing as many clients in the shortest period of time as possible. The second thing you manufacture is whatever it is that you are delivering to that client. Your team takes this new order and delivers the value you promised, in a fast and exceptional way. Neither speed nor quality can be compromised.

You'll continue this cycle of selling and delivering, again and again, to both new and existing clients.

Your existing clients will feel more comfortable making larger purchases more frequently as you complete each cycle.

With your client machine generating new clients on the front end, you can offer even more value through additional products or services, generating more revenue throughout the lifetime of the relationship. The faster you can effectively sell and the more cycles you can complete in a shorter period of time, the higher the lifetime value of each new client becomes. The increase in the number of clients, multiplied by the increase in lifetime value of each client, becomes exponential business growth.

Speed Growth by Niche

Let's get back to what this has to do with a choosing a niche, and how doing so will accelerate your growth. Many of you reading this book are business owners or executives of companies with teams of people.

To demonstrate the point, let's consider the solopreneur, a one-person operation, where time is the biggest challenge.

After proving the point as a solopreneur, it will be easy to see the impact when you multiply this to reflect a team. Suppose you're a marketing consultant hired by a dentist to create a marketing campaign for his practice. The dentist asks you to create the step-by-step process his team should follow to bring in new business. You are to create all the copy for direct mail campaigns, email, and scripts his team should use. You and the dentist agree on a fee of $15,000 for all the work you will do.

To do this effectively, you start with your discovery process, to ensure a complete understanding of his practice, including the ideal customers to target, the procedures that will be offered, pricing, and the differentiating factors that brought the existing customers to this practice.

After your discovery, you research other campaigns that dentists have used to get extraordinary results, so you can model some of those campaigns or at least pull some ideas out of them. That initial $15,000 project sounded lucrative, but you quickly start to realize the more work that goes into this, the more the value diminishes. Now it's time for you to create. You write and rewrite all the different pieces that will go into this campaign. Finally, when you think most the work is over, you still have to test. You do small mailings to test different variations of the marketing pieces to see what people are responding to, so you get the highest response rates from all your efforts. When all is said and done, you've spent two months on this project and now that it's over, it's time to find more clients.

Let's start with the capacity perspective, number 2 on our previous list: The speed of delivering the goods or services.

In the scenario above, if you're a marketing consultant without a niche then you will only be able to handle a few clients at one time. Imagine having to do a different discovery, research, writing, testing, and finalizing for every new client you have, because they come from a number of different industries. At most you'd be able to handle a few per month (effectively), limiting your income to $150-$300k a year. Keep in mind, we haven't even discussed the fact that it would take time to speak to prospects and sell before you even get the projects. Now, let's reimagine you as that marketing consultant, but focused on working exclusively with dentists. Now you have this great process which you just spent two months perfecting. It's all mapped out and you have amazing copy written for direct mail pieces, email, and even telephone or in-person scripts practices can use. Why not sell this entire system to another practice that doesn't compete with your client? What if you sold it to one dentist in every state? That's 50 clients for the work you just did for one. In fact, you can easily find two dentists per state that can't possibly serve the same demographic, because people will only travel so far from their home. The point is, from a capacity perspective, you can easily handle

100 of these clients this year. By choosing a niche, you can deliver your services better and faster, allowing you to increase your revenue to $1.5M a year (100 x $15,000).

Now let's try another scenario. Imagine your business provides detergents and soaps to chain restaurants in New York City. Your competitor sells detergents and soaps, but they sell it to anyone, anywhere.

They don't want to 'limit' themselves. This means they have accounts spread out in different locations and they sell to different types of establishments like restaurants, hotels, and catering halls.

Who do you think will sell a million dollars' worth of soap faster? From a capacity perspective, you will. For those of you not so familiar with the scene, getting in and out of New York City is time consuming and costly. Because your accounts are all consolidated in one area, you are centrally located and can deliver to all your accounts in one day while your competitor has drivers going through all five boroughs and beyond. Because you deal with just restaurant chains, your customers do volume with you, and they go through product faster with all their locations. Also, because you deal with restaurant chains, logistically delivering your product is so much easier because it's the same process for all the franchised restaurants.

Let's move on to the other very important speed benefit of choosing a niche: The speed of making a sale.

Going back to our marketing consultant example, would you expect it to be easier or harder to sell your services to another dentist, compared to let's say, an attorney? Obviously, the dentist is easier. You already have proof of concept, a testimonial, and a reference your new prospective dentist can speak to.

Can you use that same testimonial or reference for

the attorney? Sure. It just won't hold the same weight because the process you created for the dentist won't necessarily work for the attorney, who's also hoping you'll do the same great job for their industry. So how about you focus on selling this just to dentists, and now you have 10 different dentists who will speak highly of your services? Will that make things even easier when approaching the next dentist? Of course! Soon you become unstoppable. Plus, the moment you tell your prospects that you only serve the dental industry, you completely eliminate competition. No longer are you competing with every marketing consultant in the world. Now, you're only competing with marketing consultants who specialize in serving dental practices. And the great news for you is that most of your competitors are as scared of picking a niche as you once were. So, the truth is, once you do this you won't have any competition.

Dominating One Market at a Time

To create rapid growth, everyone in your business must be proactive. This is the exact opposite of what typically happens for slow growth companies. Slow growth executives constantly find themselves in a reactive state, and these reactions are what actually slow growth down. Think of the saying 'one step forward, two steps back.' Those two steps back were the result of some negative event which happened in the business, and what we call reactions are the effort we make to fix it or control the damage. But when we're constantly reacting, we're exerting as much energy as if we're moving forward, just without the progress, because all we're doing is compensating for the steps we've taken backwards. If you do this often enough, you'll feel like a hamster on a wheel.

So, to avoid that scenario, the proactive approach you need to take is to choose a niche and go down the line, piercing through that market. The top 1% in all categories go deep, rookies go wide. The big fear everyone has is that they'll miss opportunities that fall outside their market. You may still ask, "What if this additional business outside my niche finds me, while I'm hunting for the business that falls in my niche?" I'll double down and caution you that anything outside your expertise requires you to learn, which requires more of your time and that time is expensive. Getting involved in markets that are outside your wheelhouse will require you to move much slower and this extra time will cost you more revenue in comparison to sticking to your niche. Obviously, in some cases it may be irresponsible for you to turn away business, so in those cases do what you must. But throughout the process, think about what it will cost you in time to actually get the business and deliver the best possible product/service flawlessly. Anything less than the best will cost you.

The good news is that once you've dominated your market there are many different markets to expand into. You can go one-by-one, dominating each space until you've officially conquered the world. But until you've dominated one market, it wouldn't make sense to waste the effort just being a drop in another bucket. There's no benefit to spreading yourself thin. We can see how each effort can compound your business if you build upon and use all of your previous efforts. Each case study, testimonial, reference, or industry award can be used to further dominate more of that specific market. Social proof mounts until you are recognized by everyone as the leader in that market. In a world full of generalists, you'll be a specialist. And just like outdated methods of mass marketing, your competitors will still be using the antiquated approach of mass appeal, yet never appealing to anyone.

Think About One Buyer (at a Time)

In sales, you often hear phrases like, "It's a numbers game" or "On to the next one." At first, they seem innocent enough. They just sound like a positive way to stay persistent so that you don't become discouraged and give up. But be warned. These sayings originated from a mindset that would be harmful to your business or sales career if you adopted that mentality in today's business environment. This mindset attempts to compensate for something that is ineffectual, by increasing volume. This delusional and destructive mindset says it's okay to reach out to people that aren't the right fit, just as long as you reach out to enough people to get the job done. That might work for the sales manager who's stuck in 1984, but that doesn't work for all the people whose time is completely wasted, getting absolutely no value out of the exchange.

The damage isn't limited to the names on that bad

prospect list. Even more damage is being done to the salespeople facing constant rejection by a large number of unqualified people, who would never be able to give a positive response in the first place. I see this mentality every day when we get a terrible cold email written by someone who's not taken the time to learn what people respond to. Or even worse, I get an email pertaining to something that has nothing to do with us, never mind being able to add value. When these people don't get any positive responses from sending their garbage out, the only solution they come up with is, "I must need to send to a larger list".

Yes, more of something can compensate, but you want to maximize first and then multiply so that you're compounding the positive effects to get exponential results.

Mass marketing, blanketing crowds, is just as ineffective as not having a niche. Again, it's trying to appeal to everyone and never appealing to anyone. The top 1% of marketers has moved to a laser-targeted sniper approach to marketing. What would happen to your response rates if you reached out to specific people with a message that is so personal, offering a solution that seems so customized to the individual problem that person is experiencing, and using words that seem like they were only meant for them in their unique situation? Your results would go through the roof because those messages are hard to ignore. But the numbers game mentality builds a gigantic list consisting of many different market segments. In order for your copy to speak to all those different segments at once, your language has to be very generic. That general language may allow you to talk to a large number of people at once, but specifics and personalization is what actually creates interest and gets a response. So what good is speaking to everyone at once if what you're saying isn't getting anyone's interest?

At the same time, we must balance being effective with being efficient. Although a manually written ultra-personalized message may be the most effective, it would severely limit us because we only have so much time in a day. Imagine if you didn't have to compile a list at all.

Wouldn't it be great if you had some amazing piece of software that was able to analyze millions of conversations on social media, read blog posts along with the comments below, and sift through online reviews to find your next perfect prospect?

Can you imagine if you had some way of knowing who the one person is that needs your product or service more than anyone else in the world? If you were able to pinpoint with that accuracy, your sales process would be quick and easy.

With that kind of precision targeting, you wouldn't need to reach out to even one other person since you can only have one conversation at a time. And when you're done helping that person then you would move to the next highest value target.

Maybe Artificial Intelligence will get us there someday, but the point is if we could target that well, we would target the best prospects and just pick them off one at a time instead of mass marketing.

The closest thing to that technology today is to focus on that one perfect buyer and then create a profile of that person, known as a Client Avatar or Buyer Persona. It allows you to personify your target market and speak to them in a way that will resonate with your best buyers.

You can segment your lists and create a persona for

each segment. You can speak to a thousand people that fall under that one persona and yet everyone would feel like you are speaking only to them. Who are the people in your niche that you are targeting? What do you know about them? What do they like and dislike? The deeper you go in targeting, the more personalized you can make your message, directly tapping into their fears, frustrations, ambitions, and desires.

When building your personas, start with the business, and then move to the economic buyer. Consider the following factors:

- Sector
- Industry
- Company Size (# of Employees, Revenue, Market share)
- Company Age or Stage in Lifecycle
- Executive Title
- Gender

- Age Range

- Years at Company

- Responsibilities

- Goals/Objectives

- Challenges

- Interests/Passions

- Likes/Dislikes

One last thing on this topic: sometimes I see people try to create personas that are too specific and not realistic of the entire group. They create these back stories based on a couple of real life examples.

Just because two people like surfing, obviously, that doesn't mean to speak to all your prospects about the beach. But you will find some commonalities among your entire group. For example, the software industry is very sophisticated with regard to sales.

I find that most executives in the tech world continually educate themselves in the latest sales best practices. Furthermore, some executives spend more time learning sales strategies than others, just because of their day-to-day responsibilities. So, if you were to approach a sales-savvy executive such as the VP of Sales, who operates in a sales-savvy industry like SaaS, and you were to contact them using an old-school sales approach, you would expect to get a very negative response. In other words, don't expect to get anywhere using telemarketing and not taking the time to do a little research on the company. By not following certain etiquette, you will consistently fail with this buying persona.

Yet, you may use the same method to approach an executive in the manufacturing industry and you'll have better luck. Build your Buyer Personas and look for these types of observations.

Your campaigns will be much more successful because of your ultra-personalized approach and messaging.

> **Resource:** Download the Ideal Client Profile sheet that I personally use to create Client Avatars. You can download your copy at www.client-machine.com/ICP

Focus on Your Next 100 Prospects

You're building your target list and you're ready to take over the world. Using the 'Dentist' example earlier, when doing your research, you find that you can purchase a list of 154,000 dental practices across the country. In your excitement you make your purchase and you're off to the races. Great, now what? Can you afford to do a 150k+ direct mail campaign? Maybe, but even if so it wouldn't be cost effective to do one large campaign like that. Can you make 154,000 calls? No, not unless you do robocalls, and you're smart enough to know that's not the answer. Can you email that many? Yes, but again now you're back to speaking very generally when personalization is the key to getting high responses. The trick is to break down the list into small segments and the smaller the segment the more you can personalize. The goal is to focus on the first 100 prospects, speaking to one very specific persona and personalize it as much as you can.

Then you can worry about the other 153,900. The number 100 isn't a fixed rule. The rule is breaking your list up into as many small pieces as possible and to personalize the message as far as you can. Do this repeatedly.

I want to give you an example outside of our B2B world to demonstrate how important segmentation and personalization is for everyone. This especially comes into play when you're writing your outreach campaigns later. Years ago, a friend of mine had a martial arts studio and was looking to grow the business.

As a friend, and as a student that wanted the school to grow, I created multiple marketing campaigns and a sales process so that we would have a steady flow of new students enrolling. The student base started growing pretty rapidly, and within just a couple of months we needed a much larger training facility.

My buddy Chief, (short for Chief Instructor), found a facility four times the size of his original studio. The size of the new facility would allow him to continue to grow the business, but it also meant moving his school into a new city. Although there was risk in losing existing students, the move created an opportunity to market to an entire new geography and capture more customers. This new location also gave him the opportunity to offer fitness training on the days there were no martial arts classes. Those that weren't interested in martial arts, now had another reason to become a customer.

We moved to the new location and created a campaign that went door to door bringing awareness to all the local neighbors about crimes that had happened within a 10-mile radius over the past 6 months.

They were surprised to hear the number of robberies and violent crimes that were happening not too far from their homes.

The campaign goal was to bring awareness and provide solutions to protect themselves and their families. As a thank you to the new neighborhood that was welcoming us, we offered several free self-defense classes where anyone who lived in the neighborhood could learn the basics of self-defense. We provided residents with a list of emergency contact telephone numbers, and specific instructions on how to handle almost any emergency situation from home invasions to smelling smoke. Not only were the residents happy about the new self-defense gym moving into the neighborhood, but they were also happy to answer our survey questions about what was most important to them.

We asked questions like, "What appeals to you more about our new facility, self-defense training or physical fitness?" and, "Why is that important to you?"

Although going door to door speaking to people was a very time-consuming task, the data that we got from it was incredible. We knew the names, addresses, contact information, and specific preferences of hundreds of residents. For those that had no interest in self-defense but had an interest in physical fitness, they were only sent marketing on fitness and health. For the men who responded that their biggest concern was not being able to protect the women in their lives when they weren't home, they were sent marketing pieces on special training classes designed for men and women to train together. Many of these new students initially came in because of self-defense but found a new hobby that they could do together to bring them closer in their relationships. The point is that everyone has different preferences, and what appeals to some cannot possibly appeal to all. By appealing to each segment's preferences, this martial arts academy outgrew their new location in less than one year!

Could this same result have been achieved by blanketing the entire neighborhood with mailings? Sure. But that falls back on the destructive and delusional mindset that we mentioned earlier. To reference this behavior when we see it, let's call it the Numbers-Game Mentality. It represents the old school mentality of marketing and sales, where you increase the volume of your efforts in order to compensate for inefficient or ineffective practices. You may ask, "What would make it ineffective if the same result is achieved?" Let's start with my 92-year-old grandmother we call Yiayia.

Although she doesn't live in the neighborhood of the martial arts school, she represents many other elderly men and women who do live there. No matter how much crime is happening in her neighborhood, Yiayia will never be taking a self-defense class.

Again, no matter how amazing your technique to shed fat or what state-of-the-art equipment you've developed to build strength, you are not getting this cute old lady into your gym. New price promotions? It can be free and she's still not going. This means that you could send her a mailing every day for the rest of her life and you will never get her as a customer. Knowing that, would it still be worth continuing or should you just never mail her again? On the other hand, there are people in that same neighborhood that are prime prospects and just had not said YES yet. Maybe they're in a contract with their gym waiting for it to expire in a few months before they join yours. Maybe they're interested in martial arts but have a big project at work that will keep them busy, so the next two months are not good for them. They'll reconsider in the summer time. Would it make sense to never mail these prospects again just because right now is not a good for time for them to join?

Herein lies the problem with the approach followed in most people's marketing efforts. They waste resources like time, money, and energy, contacting people that will never be a good fit and will never buy, and they give up too early on the prospects that are a fit but just haven't responded yet. By segmenting your lists into tiny categories, you can stop wasting time and money on what can never work, so you have more resources to allocate to what can. The results you get will amaze you. It's said that on average people need to come in contact with a brand at least 7-9 times before making a purchase. Can you see how easy it is to blow a budget on a big list and run out of gas before you contacted all the good prospects the appropriate number of times needed to get a response? Just remember, amateurs go wide, pros go deep. One last mention, I use the word mailing in this example because of the nature of the business we described and the fact that the most obvious cost in mailings is financial. The word mailings can easily be substituted with calls, emails, or LinkedIn messages. Since most of these outreach efforts won't impact your budget at all, the resource that will be depleted most is time, which is much more expensive than money. I intentionally used an example that has a hard cost because in my experience, people don't value their time nearly as much as they value money, when realistically it's the same thing.

Why You Need to Use Research to Understand Your Market, Customers, and Competitors

"You can see a lot by just looking."

- Yogi Berra

The subject of marketing research has been known to send shivers down the spine of even experienced marketers. They view marketing research as somewhat mysterious and based on complex scientific principles and costly statistical analysis. Yet, the fact is, research doesn't have to be expensive. And you don't necessarily have to pay an outside expert to conduct research for you, although it may be prudent for you to do so.

What you must do, regardless of the size or scope of your marketing endeavors, is practice certain time-tested fundamentals. If you fail to follow these fundamentals, the data you generate may be useless, or even worse, counterproductive, because it may be inaccurate or lead you in a direction that is a danger to your business.

A Dozen Good Uses for Marketing Research

Identify new markets for products and services – Marketing research can help you find untapped audience segments for your current product and service offerings. These audience segments could be as broad as major new prospect groups or as narrow as small market niches.

Classify new business and consumer segments by their demographic, geographic, and psychographic characteristics – This is an important purpose of marketing research because you can't effectively promote to a unique audience segment until you are fully aware of its defining characteristics.

Find new uses for an existing product – A product is often shelved because it has supposedly reached the saturation point in its market penetration. Research can help you revive a product and start its life cycle all over again.

Test the viability of new products and services – Smart companies want to have an idea of the potential for a new product before spending large sums on development costs. Research can point out modifications that can save a product which would otherwise be a failure. Equally important, research can help you save considerable sums by foregoing products that have no chance of success.

Locate decision-makers and influencers – Promotions aimed at the wrong prospect are a great waste of promotional dollars. Locating the right prospect is particularly important in business-to-business marketing since there can be many people involved with the decision-making process.

Define the sales cycle – Research can help discover two important questions about the product sales cycle. First, how much time does it take from initial contact through the close of business? Second, what is the internal process that prospects go through when evaluating and purchasing products?

Reduce the risk of poor product development and marketing decisions – In a fast-changing, technical world where product life cycles can be as short as eighteen months, business executives can't afford to make major mistakes in product development or marketing. Research is a valuable tool when it comes to improving the quality of decisions.

Test your copy, graphics, offer, and message impact before your promotions are seen by the wider audience – As you will read throughout this book, millions of dollars are wasted on marketing initiatives that have no chance of success. Proper pre-testing of promotions will usually increase the chance of success. Post-testing helps refine future advertising so that it gets better over time.

Evaluate product or service benefits – It is amazing how often a company is wrong about why consumers purchase its products and services. The only way to be truly sure about the benefits and advantages of a particular product is to ask the people who know best – existing customers.

Determine brand strength and positioning versus the competition – The market is comprised of more than your company and its prospects and customers; it also includes competitors. Your position versus the competition is constantly changing, sometimes in subtle ways, and it is imperative for you to understand these changes. Marketing research can help you accomplish this goal.

Select the best media tools – Poor media selection is fatal to marketing programs. Media planners can use research to help develop media schedules that maximize the cost-effectiveness of every dollar spent on print, broadcast, direct mail, and other marketing vehicles.

Track customer satisfaction – Research can be used to get a moving picture of your customers' attitudes about your products, services, pricing, personnel, policies, and so forth. Trends spotted in customer satisfaction can be used to head off serious problems. Many companies are afraid to conduct satisfaction surveys because they are afraid customers will take this as a sign that there are problems. Actually, the reverse is true. Customers like to be asked for their opinions, and consider it a sign that a company truly wants to improve its products and services.

These are just some idea starters and you can probably come up with other uses that are specific to your business. However, the point of research is to help you make decisions that are more likely to produce desired outcomes. But you must always remember that research is a support tool, not an infallible science. Research is meant to guide, not dictate, your decisions.

Direct Mail Questionnaires

Direct mail survey projects are expensive and time-consuming so you want to make sure the mailed questionnaire is complete and not lacking in any substantive way. In certain circumstances, such as when the list does not contain telephone numbers, written questionnaires may be the only practical way of collecting the required data. To get the best response rate out of your written survey questionnaire, always adhere to the following guidelines. (Note that many of these principles also apply when you create an electronic survey.)

Make sure you interview individuals who have a genuine or perceived interest in the survey's subject matter. This is the primary consideration in the accuracy of the research data.

The questionnaire should be easy to read, both from a copy and layout standpoint. To increase legibility, always leave plenty of white space on the page.

Keep the questionnaire as short and uncomplicated as possible. It is better to do without a few questions than to go for every shred of data and risk a low response rate.

Survey research is supposed to measure how the marketplace feels about a particular subject at a certain point in time. It is a snapshot, not a moving picture. This is why you need to complete the project in a relatively short time frame, and never mix the answers of questionnaires filled out over long periods.

Always send a letter with your survey questionnaire. The letter should be personalized if possible, and convince the respondent that she is important and her answers are valuable. Even a short note on the survey form itself is better than going without a letter.

Don't forget to tell the respondent why you are conducting the survey and how the findings from the research report will benefit him in his professional and/or personal life. You must never give the impression that the person's answers will be used to try to sell him something.

Give your survey an impressive title. For example, a title such as "Survey of Important Executives in the Information Services Industry" will gain better response than one titled "Computer Industry Survey."

Assure the respondent that her participation in the research project will be held in strict confidence. If possible, allow the recipient to answer the questionnaire without revealing her name. Try not to put the person's name on the survey form itself, but, if you must, provide a way for individuals to tear it off before mailing.

If you are conducting business research, consider offering each respondent a summary report on the survey's conclusions. Assuming your list contains the names of those who have an interest in the subject matter, you should get a good response rate.

Put a live stamp on the pre-addressed return envelope. At the least, include a postage-paid business reply envelope. Never ask the recipient to pay the return postage.

If you are concerned about the response rate, use a before- and/or after-response booster.

One week before you mail the questionnaire, send a postcard notifying the subject that an important survey will be arriving shortly.

If the response rate on the first mailing is small, you can also mail a copy of the questionnaire to non-respondents with a note suggesting they may not have received the original and that you are waiting for their reply. The trick is to be expectant, but never demanding.

Consider including a premium with your questionnaire. The right premium can double or even triple response. Successful premiums include coins, dollar bills and advertising specialties such as pens and calendars. Be careful not to imply that you are buying the respondent's time with the premium, but rather are including it "as a token of appreciation."

Telephone Surveys

Telephone surveys have a number of advantages over written questionnaires. For starters, you can get the information much faster. You can develop a program, test, collect the data by phone, compile the data, and prepare follow-up reports in two to three weeks. Telephone surveys also give you a lot of flexibility. For example, perhaps you have conducted fifty phone interviews and several of your subjects raise an unexpected issue. Simply revise the questionnaire and include the new questions on all subsequent calls. This level of flexibility is not possible with written questionnaires.

Many consumers are extremely wary of telephone surveys because they have been subject to phony surveys where the real purpose of the call was to sell a product or service, instead of conducting legitimate research. Because of these abuses, and the inherent intrusive nature of the medium, a high percentage of individuals will no longer participate in telephone research. Since non-responders tend to fall into certain groups, you may not have all segments represented in your sample.

To increase the likelihood of getting your telephone questions answered, keep all questions short and simple. Unless the recipient of the call is deeply involved in the subject matter (or being paid to answer), it is very difficult to keep someone on the phone more than a few minutes. You also want to make sure you represent a cross-section of the universe in your survey. If you are using a master telephone list, don't just tear off a section of the list and start calling. You may be limiting the respondents to a certain geographic area or other segment.

Try to complete each call in a short time period and start out by informing the respondent how long the interview will last. Just as with written questionnaires, it may be better to drop a few questions in the interest of achieving a higher response rate.

Regardless of the survey media or methodology, try not to get too wrapped up in the research project. And do not let it slow you down. As Tom Peters said, you need to "Test fast, fail fast, adjust fast."

Why is business to business CE different?

The bottom line for Customer Experience is that most CEPs and approaches are based on a consumer or B2C model. Many people, including some consultants, really do not understand the fundamental difference between B2C and B2B. Several programs that have failed have done so, in large part, because of this.

In the B2C world, CE is often associated with "ease of use." Steve Jobs described the iPhone in terms of the user experience, but aspects of the Apple success story extend this to a range of aspects of the product itself—the ease of use, the flexibility of new touch-screen technology, the quality and resolution of the display, the Apple store experience, and even the "cool" packaging in which the iPhone arrives.

All of these product elements made the experience exciting and fulfilled the promises of a great experience. But the B2B world is different.

In the consumer world:

The transaction value is low (in the case of McDonald's, it is a couple dollars).

- The customer base is huge (often in the millions).

- The customers are about equal in their buying power (they all spend about the same).

- The transactions are quick and spontaneous, often based on emotion rather than reason.

- Customers have little power other than to buy or not to buy—they can rarely bargain individually, nor can they expect special discounts or faster delivery.

- Customers treat each purchase separately and base their overall view of the seller on each individual experience—one might use a restaurant for many years and then, after one bad experience, never go back.

The Customer Experience then is geared toward individual transactions, and vendors can (and should) use "big data" based on, in some cases, millions of transactions to predict how the selling process and the use can be incrementally improved.

The B2B world is very different: Larger transaction value

The average transaction value is high. Other than buying a home, the highest purchase for a consumer is an automobile. In the B2B world, products and services can be purchased for hundreds of thousands or even millions of dollars.

Smaller number of customers

Even when a company is selling to small businesses, their customer base is typically in the thousands rather than the millions.

80/20 rule-based

Not all B2B customers are equal. McDonald's spend per customer is fairly flat. In B2B, some companies and governments can spend orders of magnitude more than other, smaller companies.

The 80/20 rule applies to B2B. Developed originally by the Italian economist Pareto, this rule observes that 80% of the spend will be from just 20% of customers, with the other 20% spread over the other 80% of customers.

This allows, and requires, that companies focus on the 20%—their largest customers. Companies need to segment their customer base so that Customer Experience is resourced more to the more important customers and less to the less important ones.

In the Customer Experience Program, it is fundamental that you separate the two (or more) groups of customers and treat them separately—and measure them separately.

Often a direct sales force with vested interests

Certainly when you buy a car, there is an assertive salesperson. But because they only sell a car to an individual every few or more years, they do not focus on building and growing a relationship.

In B2B, building the relationship is most important and is the basis for the Customer Experience.

This is often done with account teams or salespeople who nurture the relationship and, in many cases, spend time learning the customer's business, challenges, and problems.

The B2B sales teams, however, usually have a vested interest in keeping management and others away from their customer contacts. In addition, as with the car salespeople, they are very keen to receive high customer-satisfaction scores, and when there is a problem with the account, they will attempt to find reasons to prevent the satisfaction interview from taking place.

Longer lead time

In a B2C environment, the lead time is usually short. Someone may search the Internet for a product, compare a few, get the best price, and buy it. It may be delivered the next day and be in use immediately. In a retail experience, the lead time may be even shorter.

For B2B, an RFP is often drawn up, approved, and sent out to qualified vendors who submit proposals. These are considered, recommendations are made, management submits approvals, and finally a purchase is made—perhaps with a significant time before delivery and implementation. This can take months or even years.

"Professional" buying

In a B2C environment, the buyer is an individual who will assess the product and price and then purchase. In B2B, there are a number of people involved, and in the past few years, more and more have come to use a professional purchasing group. Purchasing has only one task—negotiate the lowest price. Often their bonuses are set on the basis of savings they have been able to extract from their suppliers.

We have not found a case where these people are included in customer satisfaction programs whereas they often make the final decision. Even though this is likely to be based greatly on price, their input in the satisfaction measurement is important.

Complexity of the products

Along with the high unit prices and the long lead time to decision, many B2B sales are of complex products that can take a long time to implement. Sometimes the implementation process is expected to be difficult and requires the customer to have certain skills or to use outside contractors to assist.

In addition, the people who will use the product have often not been involved in the decision making, which is rare in the B2C world.

Fundamentally different decision-making process and organization

When consumers buy, they may consult friends or other family members, but usually there is just one decision maker. In a B2B situation, there are usually multiple people involved—a technical recommender, the end user, purchasing, finance, legal, and executives. The purchase may be ad hoc, but more than likely it will use funding from a budget.

Is it any surprise that a CEO with a consumer background can flounder in B2B and vice versa? Is it also any surprise that the packaged approaches to CE based on a B2C model do not play well in the B2B space?

Companies with hybrid B2B and B2C models

Many companies are hybrids—some products are sold to consumers and others to businesses (e.g., electric generators).

One of the things that causes a CEP to fail is when a company uses one approach for both consumers and B2B. The approach to each has to be different. This is a clear case when "one size does NOT fit all."

What is a CE program in B2B and why is it so complex?

A B2C Customer Experience is fairly simple.

Picture a lemonade stand. The business model is simple: the little girl provides lemonade from a lemonade stand for cash.

The Customer Experience is singular and short. The experience relates to the little girl selling the lemonade and might be expressed as:

- Friendly
- Clean
- Good quality product
- Acceptable price
- Good location
- Nice glasses to drink from
- Cute little girl

The experience also stretches out a little to include "word of mouth," signs, and local advertisements on notice boards. It also includes comparisons with other lemonade stands and memories of the little girls in other activities.

But many consumer products have a more complex Customer Experience. Let's consider the iPhone. What are the experiences that a potential buyer has? These relate to touch points. He/she might:

- Read a Wall Street Journal article about the new iPhone
- Go to Apple's website
- Watch an interview with Tim Cook
- Use the iTunes website
- Listen while a friend "talks up" the new iPhone
- Visit an Apple retail store
- Check out a competitive smart phone in a carrier store
- See a TV show about manufacturing facilities in China
- See a news program about the new iPhone
- Buy the iPhone
- Sign up for a network plan
- Activate the phone

- Use the iPhone

What impact will a negative experience at the Apple store have? Will difficulties in transferring iTunes files to a new PC affect the new iPhone purchase? If the network plan sign-up is difficult, does this impact the customer's view of Apple?

In both these cases, there is a single product and a single buyer (although peers may have an influence). The complexity comes from the product's "touch points."

In the B2B world, there are often multiple products and multiple touch points adding complexity. There is also another dimension of complexity in the roles within the customer organization that contribute to the total experience. There are many people or roles involved in the experience at the customer end—not just the "decision maker."

As well as the many products, touch points, and roles that affect the perception of the experience, there are two other aspects—the customer journey and the position of the products in their life cycle. A customer may be approaching the product purchase for the first time and will need to understand the product category and what the options are. Other customers may be well down the "journey" path and be concentrating on aspects of usage. While each customer may be at different points, the product overall will be at a point in its life cycle—embryonic, growth, mature, or decline—and the importance of the various touch points will be different based on this factor. In the embryonic stage, concentration is needed in the early customer journey steps. As the product matures, these become less important unless the vendor is targeting new users in, say, a mature market.

The B2B complexity with four dimensions

Many people/roles in the customer organization
Buyers/decision makers
Procurement
Users
Managers
Finance
Legal
C-suite executives

Many touch points
Sales people
Channels
Web site
Advertisements
PR
Peer opinions
Blogs
Consultants
Social networking

Many product sets

Customer Journey and Life cycle

I said it wasn't easy!

When we address CE, we have to review all the dimensions, and we can do that from any angle.

For one company, we developed an approach revolving around the customer journey product and the product life cycle. We first positioned each of the vendor's products against the elements of the relevant customer journey and then applied importance based on the position in the life cycle. The chart below, for product x, sets this out with the weight of the line showing those journey elements that are most important. Product x is mature, so the most important aspects were delivery and implementation and use, with less important factors in the earlier parts of the life cycle.

Different product/service sets will require different emphasis in the customer journey based on stage of maturity

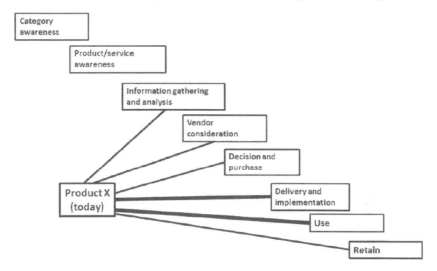

We then considered the role dimension. In the second chart we depicted where a chief marketing officer interfaces—in the very early days of an embryonic product and then in the use of the product. They do not gather information on the product that might be used (a CRM system), nor do they have any influence on the vendor consideration.

Each "player" in the customer organization has a different focus

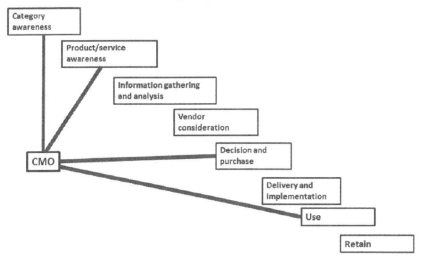

The third chart shows an analysis by a specific touch point—in this case, the website. This is used mostly during the early stages of the customer journey and the early stages in the product life cycle.

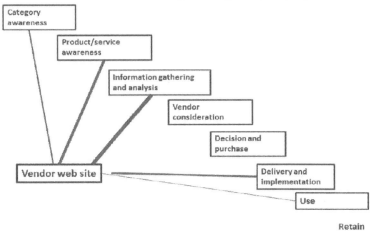

Each touch point can have different emphasis based on customer journey and life cycle

Category awareness

Product/service awareness

Information gathering and analysis

Vendor consideration

Decision and purchase

Delivery and implementation

Vendor web site

Use

Retain

These dimensions become the framework for our CE Program.

Social media and big data in Customer Experience

Many articles on Customer Experience today point out the importance of social media in understanding the Customer Experience. They then go on to point out how blogs, tweets, etc. can be analyzed using text analytics software and other "big data" approaches. This is just fine in the B2C world, but it is less useful in the B2B world. We address this further in 4.

The elements of a CEF

There are three major parts to the introduction of a successful CEP:

1. Customer focus – embedding the customer in the vendor's culture and strategies

2. The framework within which the program will be rolled out

3. Implementation – measurement, the actions to take optimal corrective action, and feedback to the customers

The focus on Customer Experience needs to be part of the company culture—it is not just paying lip service to this. Everyone in the vendor's organization should be thinking and asking the question, "What will we do to make the Customer Experience better?"

Customer Experience needs to be built into the strategy of the company and then into product or business unit strategies and tactics.

There needs to be a framework to which the strategies and measurement aspects are anchored.

- A holistic view of the customer (and prospects) – who are they, and what are their behaviors, attitudes, needs, and wants?
- Customer sets – what are the logical groupings for our customers? Based on size? Revenue to us? Margin?
- What roles are important in the customer organizations – this is of little importance in

B2C, but for B2B it is fundamental and is often missed by traditional customer satisfaction programs. It goes beyond just the buyer and includes users, procurement, legal, and senior executives.

- Touch points – what are the specific touch points we use to provide the Customer Experience (e.g., direct sales people, website, call center)?

- Customer journey – the progression in the Customer Experience for an individual customer

- Life cycle portfolio – the experience requirements will be different at different phases in the product life cycle.

The implementation starts with measuring activities in terms of the customer's view of the experience. The traditional methods of market research work well here, but there are other methods that can be added.

Following identification of problems (either one-off or systemic), there needs to be an optimization of the actions to be taken to resolve them. The actions need to be tracked to ensure that they are effective, and future measurement with customers is necessary to verify the fixes.

Finally feedback is required to the customers. They need to be told that their comments have been heard and acted on. If the problem cannot be resolved for whatever reason, feedback regarding what was considered and then rejected can still be communicated and is far better than just ignoring the complaint.

A vendor's embrace of CE is across a continuum. It can be anywhere from a simple customer satisfaction study run once a year to a total CEP (where the customer satisfaction methodology is used for one part of the program—to gain feedback from customers). What is missing from this is the experience with the product over time, the experience in the customer journey to using the product—awareness, consideration, alternatives, plus the various touch points (e.g., customer service a few weeks in when the product has a problem or something cannot be made to work). Customer satisfaction relies on a simple survey methodology and can be invasive.

CE covers the whole life cycle, the whole set of touch points, the whole product and service set from the vendor (including its interaction) and all the players who are involved. It should go beyond the traditional survey and accept inputs from a wide variety of sources (e.g., customer service, the sales force, automated responses, social media, and web scanning).

No wonder it isn't easy.

Currently CE is fragmented

Few, if any, vendors operate without some form of customer focus. Advancing that to a full CEP has taken a number of different paths, and sometimes, the resulting program is not optimal since some of the logical steps have been missed or have been implemented without the CEP concept in mind.

There is an old Irish joke with the punch line, "You know, sir, if I was going to Balbriggan, I wouldn't start from here at all." *Source: http://www.abitoblarney.com/irishjokes.htm*

In the same way, to get to a full CEP, the path will usually be determined from the starting point.

Most B2B CEPs that we have observed are outgrowths from a customer satisfaction program. This is both positive and negative.

On the positive front, there is an organization already in place that can implement the next spin, and a lot of the mechanics for determining the customer viewpoint are already in place. If the customer satisfaction program is well accepted and used to make changes in the organization—with the customer satisfaction management having a "seat at the table" in executive discussions—the transition is easier. If the customer satisfaction approach is not held in great regard and is viewed as a low-cost way of creating a "feel good" scorecard and little else, it may be better to start from another angle and, at a suitable time, transition the existing approach.

One company that develops software for electronic circuit design has taken a different approach.

The CEO infused in all employees a set of customer-centric systems, processes, and culture. He adopted a five-part strategy focusing on areas he believed were the main challenges for his company. These were not discovered from market research but by internal workshops with the account teams. In fact, their customers were chip makers and very limited in numbers.

The areas for the CEP were related to touch points:

- Customer education
- Online customer portal
- Support centers
- Field application engineers
- Professional services organization

An initial "diagnostic study" was used to determine the metrics against which each of these could be measured.

The program was managed through a central CRM system and was recognized as a partial solution. The existing customer satisfaction program was adapted to provide ongoing measurement of the program.

Customer Focus

It would take a very foolhardy CEO to assert that the customer is not important. Going back a century or so, salespeople were exhorted with the phrase, "The customer is king," and this philosophy has continued. Indeed, one CEO of a lower-end retail jewelry chain in the UK joked at a company dinner that his company's products were "crap" and their customers were stupid for buying them. The media picked up the story, and the CEO was fired within two weeks.

Most CEOs will say they are customer focused, but this is not a black or white situation.
Some vendors fully embrace the customer while others do so to a lesser extent.

Where they lie on the spectrum of customer focus is the important aspect and leads to the level of Customer Experience Program that is most appropriate for the vendor.

Interestingly, Apple has positioned itself as a product-driven company. They will engineer and deliver the best technology with a great user experience. Of course, the customer is fundamental, but they believe that they can provide products the customers will love. This "build the field and they will come" philosophy has obviously been highly successful.

The CEP has to be in line with the philosophy and culture of the vendor. If a new CEO wishes to change the culture of the company he/she is coming into, the CEP can play an important role in making the change, or it can operate against a philosophy already in place.

The absolute first step in developing or modifying a CEP is to understand where the company is (or wishes to be) on the customer focus spectrum. In the B2C marketplace, there are few, if any, situations where a small number of customers dominate sales. Customer focus can be a more mechanical approach. In B2B, getting the customer focus right is fundamental.

The CEO tends to be focused on internals—people, organization structure, etc.—and he/she must focus down onto two or three major simple issues: quality and throughput, low-cost producer, best marketer of financial services for selected target customers, or superior branch network, for example. Or "the Customer Experience."

The following transcript is from a 60 Minutes episode on Amazon that aired on Dec. 1, 2013. Charlie Rose is the correspondent who interviewed Jeff Bezos, CEO of Amazon.

Charlie Rose: Tell me what is Amazon today?

Jeff Bezos: I would define Amazon by our big ideas, which are customer centricity, putting the customer at the center of everything we do, and invention. We like to pioneer, we like to explore, we like to go down dark alleys and see what's on the other side.

The customer focus index

So where is your company on the customer focus continuum?

We have asked vendors to position themselves on this simple 1-7 scale.

Score	Our beliefs relating to the customer	Our attitude towards customers	Appropriate program
1	We dominate our marketplace and our customers have to buy from us. We place little focus on our customers	They are a pain in the a***	Low level customer satisfaction program conducted once every few years
2	Our customers are important to us but we do not use their input to determine our actions and strategy	They pay the bills so we have to put up with them	
3	Our customers are important to us and we measure customer satisfaction. We do not rely on input from them to drive our company strategy	We need to keep our costs down in dealing with customers	
4	We track customers and take what they tell us seriously. We use a scorecard to determine how well we are doing	We try to keep them happy and use basic satisfaction programs	Continuous customer satisfaction program
5	We have a strong relational dialog with our customers but position ourselves as leading them rather than them dictating what we do	We have programs in place to track their satisfaction and loyalty levels and we act on their issues	
6	Customer experience in in our top three areas of focus	We maintain an active dialog with our customers to understand them and their needs	
7	We are totally responsive to our customers in terms of products, service, marketing,. We rely on their continuous input to evolve our business	Pleasing them is the most important goal we have as a company	Full CEP

131

Obviously different people in the vendor organization will have different views, and the collecting of these different views makes for an invaluable exercise. We recommend that the data be collected in a structured, quantitative manner so that analysis can be undertaken across geographies, functional units, management hierarchy, etc. The differences will allow action to be taken to reinforce the CEO's fundamental view. If he/she believes that the vendor is a type 6 company, and the sales force believes that the company operates as a type 3 company, there is a lot of realignment to be done.

The survey needs to cover all groups and functions within the company.

Let's now address the three areas of customer focus:

- Culture
- Corporate strategy
- Product strategy and tactics

The Culture

A customer-centric culture is an engrained belief across the vendor that the customer is fundamental to the success of the company. In some vendors, lip service is paid to this, and the culture reverts to doing the least possible to "keep the customers happy" rather than embracing the relationship with the customers to provide value for both sides.

Culture is an emotional aspect, and it can be very difficult to change this. Sometimes, however, something simple can bring about the change.

Most American airlines have been through significant turbulence in their fortunes, and in many cases this has affected the attitude of their people. The result has been that those interacting with their business (and consumer) customers do not provide the expected service levels and, even more important, the expected attitude. The flight attendants have seen pay cuts and have responded by regarding their jobs as mundane and disrespected by management.

Many years back, flying was fun. The flight attendants were happy and wanted to do everything they could to make the passengers' flight enjoyable. This is a "culture thing." The flight attendants are no longer hired and trained to bring that attitude to their work. Exceptions can be found in the newer airlines like JetBlue and Southwestern, which from the beginning have embraced the "enjoyable service" culture.

In terms of changing culture, some years ago, British Airways moved through a period when a customer-centric attitude was not part of their culture, and they lost market share to Virgin Atlantic and other airlines. They changed. A strong message came down from the executive office that this was expected and that the customer was fundamental to the airline's success. The change happened almost overnight. Part of the rapid acceptance was that employees like to have their customers happy rather than miserable. It is up to management to embrace the customer focus and then support it with actions. The "nickel and diming" that has gone on in a lot of the airlines supports the belief that the customer is unimportant to the airline.

While there are a few situations where the company culture is not driven by the beliefs of the CEO, this is rare.

Typically, it is the CEO who establishes the culture. But that person must ensure that the concept is not just held in the corporate offices or the boardroom but spread throughout the company and supported by appropriate actions. The phrase all of us hear a lot when contacting customer service is, "Your call is important to us," followed by a complex IVR system and eventually an agent who has been recruited based on low cost rather than expertise, experience, and attitude. This is a classic example of how the actions do not match the message.

It is difficult for an entrenched CEO to bring about a change in culture, even if it revolves around customer centricity.

It is much easier when a new CEO comes into a company. If he/she finds a well-entrenched culture, the options are to embrace the existing, make minor changes that can be become more major changes over time, or make a radical change. If the company is in trouble before the new CEO joins, he/she will have a greater and more defensible ability to make the changes.

Culture relates to values, beliefs, and attitudes, so influencing and changing this can be difficult. There are also questions regarding how ethical it is to try to change it. However, behavior is something different. This can legitimately be changed by training and by incentive. Telling staff that they should embrace the customer and do everything to make their experience better may not fly with some people, but providing incentives such as an award for the most customer focused person of the week, etc. can support the behavior that a customer focused company requires. To introduce a customer focus culture, the CEO needs to prepare the principles of behavior into a written document that is distributed across the organization. This needs to be followed by education in small groups, workshops, etc. A CE spokesperson may even join all the strategy sessions and continue to ask the question, "How does that improve the Customer Experience?" This is a little like the slave in ancient Roman triumph parades who would continually say, "Memento mori"—you are only mortal—to the honored general to ensure that the triumph did not go to his head.

Reward systems are fundamental, but there is a risk that managers will attempt to "game the system" rather than embrace the culture that is being implemented. When managers' bonuses are impacted by Customer Experience or customer satisfaction scores, there can be some harmful byproducts.

Nurturing and convert

In this phase of the marketing funnel, each captured lead is nurtured through informative marketing with the goal of converting it to an opportunity.

Assessing potential of new leads

There are two factors that determine the revenue potential of a new lead:

- Size of the potential deal

- Likelihood of conversion from lead to customer

- Priority handling of new leads depends on its revenue potential, which in turn depends on the combination of the above two factors.

- Size of the potential deal

This metric can be estimated based on firmographic variables, like employee size, geography (especially country), industry and annual revenue. The best way to quantify this would be by a regression analysis using the list of customers connecting their initial ARRs with all key firmographic variables. This will allow us to predict potential ARR of a new lead, given the above variables.

If such thorough analysis is not feasible, one can use a simplified methodology with the "number of employees" as the independent variable that predicts the ARR. In fact, many SaaS companies have created a tiered sales and marketing structure based on the number of employees at the prospective company because of this reason. These tiers can include classifications such as enterprises, mid-sized businesses and small businesses. When a new lead is created, it is forwarded to the right tier based on the number of employees in the prospect company.

Likelihood of conversion

The likelihood of conversion from lead to customer is also dependent on firmographic variables. There are two ways to assess this metric. One involves a data mining analysis of past leads and those converted to wins (or opportunities, if the number of wins is too small). This will involve creating a probability function using firmographic variables, including the technologies used by the company.

However, just like we discussed for deal size, there is a shortcut to determine this likelihood if sophisticated prediction is beyond your reach. You can simply look at lead sources. Do a cohort analysis of leads generated in the past and their sources and rank which one converted to opportunities (this topic is discussed in Section 2.3). Leads from such top lead sources should be considered a "high likelihood to convert" and be treated on priority basis, as detailed in the next section.

Tips for Prioritized Handling

As we discussed earlier, the potential value of a lead is:

Size of the potential deal * Likelihood of conversion from lead to win

Ideally, handling of the leads is prioritized using the above formula and the leads are routed based on their order of importance, with the top tier getting immediate personal attention from sales and the bottom ones going to the email nurturing process.

As we discussed, calculating such a formula for every incoming lead for most companies would be cumbersome.

Therefore, more simplified lead handling can be used, as shown below:

Sales team is tiered according to the potential size of the deal (typically using the proxy "number of employees" in the prospect company). The number of tiers will depend on your business. For example: enterprise (over 1,000 employees) and mid-sized (<1,000 employees).

Leads are routed to the right tier based on the lead created.

The next item is the priority by which each lead is handled. Within each tier, the priority is differentiated as follows:

Highest priority leads, say originating from high-converting lead sources, are sent to dedicated SDRs (even directly to Account Execs at some companies).

Medium-priority leads (in the middle of lead source priority list) are sent to SDR calling queues.

Lower-priority leads are input to email nurturing program. Leads are nurtured till they attain a certain lead score and, at this point, they are routed to SDRs.

The above framework provides a lot of flexibility to meet the unique needs of your business. However, the fundamental building blocks—such as the size of the potential deal and likelihood of conversion—must be considered while formulating a prioritized handling framework for leads.

Using recycled leads to compensate for lead shortage

As you may know, the input to the marketing funnel comprises (1) new leads and (2) reopened leads. (Reopened leads are created when nurtured leads in the recycled leads database accumulate a predetermined lead score.) Both the new leads and reopened leads go through the top of the funnel and middle of the funnel stages before potential conversion to opportunities.

Marketing has targets in every quarter for the number of total leads to be created. It is possible that in some quarters the number of leads created falls short of the set goal. The good news is that there is a temporary fix for this gap — which is to find high-potential segments in recycled leads.

Recycled leads are mainly comprised of the following:

Leads that were called on by sales and were determined not yet ready for sales.

Leads that were nurtured through a drip campaign and reached the end of the automated flow without acquiring sufficient lead scores to be opened to sales rep.

Note that even the best recycled leads are not going to perform (convert) as well as new or organically reopened leads. However, it can be close to those fresher leads in performance. The main goal here is to meet the possible demand from sales for more leads.

The methodology involves the following steps:

Step 1: Identify the recycled leads that are the most similar to your customer base. The sophisticated way to do this is to perform the "Nearest Neighbor" analysis on the recycled leads. This will involve compiling a firmographic profile of current customers and using it as a target to rank the recycled leads. If such data mining analysis is not possible, use basic firmographic reporting to determine what firmographic variables are over-indexed in the customer base, and use this information to derive a segmenting plan (that uses a combination of over-indexed dimensions) to select from recycled leads. An example of over-indexing is given below:

Say the proportion of your recycled database by number of employees is as follows:

1–1,000:   70 percent

1,001–3,000:20 percent

3,000+:   10 percent

Similarly, say the proportions in your customer base is as follows:

1–1,000:   60 percent

1,001–3,000:30 percent

3,000+:   10 percent

In the above example, employee size of 1,001–3,000 is over-indexed in your customer base (index of 30 percent/20 percent of 1.5). Similarly, employee size of 1–1,000 is under-indexed and 3,000+ is even.

One example of over-indexed segmentation would be "companies with employees between 1,001 and 3,000 in the software industry."

Step 2: You can further prioritize the segments based upon recent behavior — i.e., which leads have been more active recently. More recent activity could imply higher potential for conversion.

Once the segments and priority of recycled leads is created, try reactivation tactics to get these leads back into active funnel. These tactics could include:

A calling campaign by SDRs (using an external SDR agency might be useful here).

High-touch marketing: For example, ask the recipients to fill out a survey to get a gift card (or qualify for a grand prize). The survey could be designed so that you get insights on the recipient's real need for your solution and the approximate timeline for that solution.

This methodology could come in handy from time to time when new leads are tough to come by.

Estimate funnel velocity and conversion by sources

Understanding lead funnel dynamics is a big part of B2B marketing. Two key metrics explaining the lead funnel dynamics are: Lead Velocity (how fast the lead is moving between stages) and Lead Conversion (what fraction of leads is progressing to the next stage).

One can see these two metrics are interconnected — leads with higher velocities tend to have higher conversions.

To derive the underlying analytics, one needs to use a cohort analysis technique. This involves tracking a group (of leads) across time to analyze their past or future transitions. The methodologies to be used for the two metrics are as follows:

Lead Velocity: Identify the new wins in a specific time period and track them backward to find when the corresponding leads were created and when they became opportunities.

Lead Conversion: Identify the new leads created in a set time period and look forward to find out how many of them became opportunities, and later became wins.

Let's take a closer look at both areas.

Lead Velocity

As mentioned, the approach to estimate lead velocity is to select a cohort of new wins and look backward to find time durations. Ideally you will select one full quarter's cohort of new wins (ideally the last full quarter). This is because frequency of wins varies across the quarter with more wins occurring towards the end of the quarter, and we need to consider all the wins in the quarter to get the complete picture.

The best source to get lead velocity data is lead conversion reports (generally available in CRMs like salesforce). Create such a lead conversion report with the criterion "closed-won date of last quarter". The report should contain the following three fields as a minimum:

- Lead creation date
- Opportunity creation date
- Closed-won date

In the report, only include the new leads created and remove "reopened" leads (because they will skew the results). Also, as the sample size permits, only consider the records having all the three dates mentioned above populated.

Use the above methodology to create a final report as shown below. (You can add other dimensions like lead source detail or campaign to this report as you prefer.)

Lead Velocity report template

Lead Source	Duration in days		
	Lead to Opp	Opp to Win	Lead to Win
Partner referrals			
Website inbound			
Customer referrals			
Sales prospecting			
Webinars			
Content syndication			
Virtual events			
Events / Tradeshows			
List Purchase			
Overall			

The lead sources shown in the above report are for discussion purposes only — you may have a different set of lead sources. Also, note the metric "Lead to Opportunity" is in Marketing's domain, while "Opportunity to Win" is (mostly) in Sales' domain. "Lead to Win" duration is the sum of the first two columns.

You will see a wide variation in lead velocities across different Lead Sources, with sources such as "Website Inbound" and "Partner Referrals" with much shorter durations (and higher velocities) than sources like "Events/Tradeshows" and "List Purchase".

One major use of a lead velocity report is to educate the sales department as well as company executives on the time it takes for a lead to become an opportunity and later a win. This will (hopefully) alleviate demand from sales for more leads—since generating new leads likely won't solve the problem in this quarter—and shift the selling focus to converting the existing leads.

Lead Conversion

This metric is also derived from lead conversion reports in the CRM. However, the cohort to be selected for the derivation is different—it should be leads created in a full quarter some time ago. However, if the quarter selected is too recent, leads from many slower velocity lead sources would not have a chance to convert by the time of the analysis, thereby distorting the results.

A rule of thumb for cohort time selection is as follows: If the average lead to win duration is X days, give at least 2X days as the gap between the end of the cohort quarter and analysis time. For example, if X is 90 days, give at least 180 days from end of the cohort quarter till present; this will allow for the conversion of most of the leads from your various sources.

As in the case of lead velocity calculation, make sure the following three fields are included in the report.

Lead creation date

Opportunity creation date (or an indicator that opportunity got created)

Closed-won date (or an indicator for win)

Use the above information to formulate the final report as below.

Lead Conversion report template

Lead Source	No of Leads	No of Opps	No of Wins	Lead to Opp conversion percent	Lead to Win conversion percent
Partner referrals					
Website inbound					
Customer referrals					
Sales prospecting					
Webinars					
Content syndication					
Virtual events					
Events / Tradeshows					
List Purchase					
Overall					

Here is an example: Suppose there were 10,000 leads created in the quarter selected. Then say 1,000 of them became opportunities at the analysis time (Lead to Opp conversion of 10 percent), and 100 of them became wins (Lead to Win conversion of 1 percent).

Just like lead velocity, lead conversion will also vary by lead source.

The insights gained from lead velocity and lead conversion reports will allow you to allocate more marketing focus on higher-performing lead sources.

Eestablish and refine lead score framework

Lead score is an essential metric in business-to-business marketing and sales processes. Lead score indicates the potential of a lead to convert to a sale—and therefore dictates how a lead should be handled on its way to sales.

Typically lead scoring framework contains the following two components:

These variable scores are typically positive, but they can be negative as well. An example of a negative demographic variable would be submission of a generic email instead of a company email. Examples of negative behavioral variables include opting out of emails, a period of inactivity and unanswered phone calls.

Once a lead is created, its demographic score does not undergo much change later (assuming all the demographic fields were populated). However, behavioral scores can change as the prospect gets more interested in your business and visits more webpages and downloads more content.

If you are implementing a lead score framework for the first time, you may be wondering how to start with component variable scores. The key is to start small, with few variables, and expand as you get a feel for what is important for your business.

Your marketing automation vendor is a good resource to call upon to get initial variable lead scores for companies like yours. Then work with your sales team and refine these initial scores over time.

Another good practice is to cap totals of both demographic and behavioral lead scores so that one does not dominate the other. For example, a maximum of 100 for demographic and 100 for behavioral score totals is a good plan.

For behavioral scores, the deeper into the marketing funnel a given activity is associated, the higher its lead score. For example, top of the funnel activities like visiting the homepage, opening emails and watching a short video will get low scores (say 1 or 2). In contrast, bottom of the funnel activities like visiting the pricing page, downloading a whitepaper or attending a product demo will receive much higher lead scores (say 5 or 10).

A key milestone in the marketing funnel is the score at which the lead reaches the Marketing Qualified Lead (MQL) stage. This is the stage at which the lead is ready to be handed over to sales (typically the SDR). If this threshold score is chosen correctly, the lead will be ready for a conversation and thus less likely to be flagged as "not ready." If there are too many "not ready" statuses following initial calls, the MQL score needs to be adjusted up (or variable scores need to be adjusted down). Working together with the sales team on a continual basis is vital for such adjustments.

Once you have the preliminary lead score framework established, you can refine the scoring system using real insights. After the end of a quarter is a good time to do the refinements so you have full quarter's worth of data to look at. The following guidelines will help:

Create a table with lists of campaigns and related

Campaign Name	Leads Touched	Lead Touched and Converted to Opportunity	Conversion Ratio

leads and opportunities (as in the table below). This will give an idea of which campaigns were the most effective in converting a lead to opportunity.

Campaigns that have higher conversion ratios imply underlying variables (behaviors) that should have higher scores associated. Use this to normalize variable lead scores on a quarterly basis.

From your leads database, create a frequency chart with lead score ranges in x-axis (like 0-9, 10-19, etc.) and number of leads in the y-axis. If you have a perfect lead score framework, this chart will look like a normal distribution. If not, see what changes you can make to lead scores to make the distribution closer to normal distribution.

Look at all new opportunities created the previous quarter (if too many, use a random sample) and see the demographic and behavioral traits of each corresponding lead. Have a working meeting with sales to discuss the common traits of high-performing (and low-performing) leads and adjust lead scores of variables up or down.

It's also important to create a written record of the lead score changes over time so there can be a self-correction mechanism in the future.

Final Thoughts: The Path to More Revenue

Writing this book (my sixth) has been a large undertaking but also a unique pleasure. As mentioned at the beginning, my intention was to cover the four primary ways to boost revenue:

Sell your stuff to more customers.

Sell more stuff to each customer.

Sell the same stuff for more money.

Sell stuff more often to each customer.

Yes, there are other methods (e.g. mergers and acquisitions), but if you focus your attention on these four objectives, you will be in great shape.

We've covered a lot of ground in these pages including branding, revenue models, lead-to-revenue, content, sales transformation, and much more. The six foundation strategies (Sections 3-8) will give you a strong base to grow from, and the proven tactics in Section 9 provide you with actions you can begin taking immediately to boost revenue.

The following page talks about my background and how I can help your company reach its revenue objectives. I hope to hear from you and wish you great success on your revenue growth journey.

NOTES:

NOTES:

NOTES:

NOTES:

NOTES:

Made in the USA
San Bernardino, CA
07 January 2019